Against All

True stories about (........g adversity and building resilience

Introduction by
Itayi Garande

Contributing authors

Dr Jossine Abrahams
Elizabeth Saji
Nyasha Muradzikwa
Tendai Chirima
Yulia Sukhanova
Dylan-Taf Ben
Gail Hannock

DEAN THOMPSON

Publishing

ISBN: 9798580925943

Contact Itayi Garande

Telephone: +44 7342372235
Email: itayig@hotmail.com
Website: www.deanthompson.co.uk
Website: www.itayigarande.com

CONTENTS

Introduction

Resilience is the ability to withstand adversity and bounce back from difficult life events.

Being *resilient* does not mean that people do not experience stress, emotional upheaval and suffering. Rather, an inner trait helps them adapt to changing situations and keep moving forward.

Floating down the river of time, each one of us will meet our own set of obstacles, hurdles and difficulties. How we overcome them or deal with them is based on our resilience.

This book has some inspiring and interesting, but sometimes heart-wrenching stories of struggle and navigating through the challenges that life may bring us.

From Jossine's struggle and success in spite of domestic abuse, through Elizabeth's betrayal, to Dylan-Taf's uprooting from a world that he was born in, to reaching for the stars in Europe, this book chronicles memorable and vivid true stories of resilience that will shock you and inspire you at the same time.

Take a moment to read these stories of incredible resilience which eight incredible writers I am honoured to know so bravely share. Such stories should never stay hidden and forgotten. Life is not obligingly neat. It is a series of challenges that are constantly being faced, but also constantly being resolved.

In this period of Covid19, this book is a timely intervention. We must all stay relentless in challenging and overcoming adversity. No problem lasts forever.

We must always rise up and highlight the legacy of resilience of people who found "ways out of no way". We must highlight stories such as the ones in this book, which sometimes die in the internal memories of those who never dare to speak up and share.

The importance of this book is to make sure those who face pain and suffering, in particular our children and women, do not get consumed by fear and despair and give up.

The Covid19 pandemic is unprecedented and the triage globally will be long lasting and will inflict pain on all of us, making our struggles even worse.

If history is a mirror, we can also expect that in times of crisis there will be desperate efforts to hold onto yesterday, blaming each other and not finding solutions to progress as people.

Put simply, challenges morph and change shape. It is our attitude to struggles that matters. We will have to continue to be resilient in the face of fear and despair.

At the same time, crisis provides opportunity for us to change, to recondition and change our lives.

This book represents a milestone. It is about breaking habits that have paralysed our children, our women, our communities and us. The contributors use the power of words and the power of writing to inspire others. When you succeed in life, find time to light other people's fire so that when your fire goes out, they can also return the favour and light your fire back. There is a risk of darkness if you are the only fire available.

So when you feel hopeless, always remember that there are others who have faced the problems you face today. They have overcome them. They have become resilient and have the tools to help you. Read their stories and get inspired. Every failed experiment is a step closer to success.

Do not give up. Those roadblocks, detours, obstacles and 'failures' are probably just things that are protecting you from people and places that are no meant for you.

Life is a book. You only find out the full and true picture right at the end. Just try to make sure that all the chapters in your life lead to one happy conclusion, otherwise they will lead to one big disaster.

Once you become resilient and fearless, life becomes limitless.

Itayi Garande
Editor
Dean Thompson Publishing

Amazon No. 1 Bestselling books
- *Reconditioning: Change your life in one minute*
- *Shattered Heart: Overcoming Death, Loss, Breakup and Separation*
- *Broken Families: How to get rid of toxic people and live a purposeful life*

Contact details
itayi@itayigarande.com
www.itayigarande.com
www.deanthompson.co.uk

Dedication

This book is dedicated to all those people who are bold enough to tell their stories of struggle in order to inspire others.

Silence is the ultimate betrayal. Knowledge is power and sharing is caring.

We create strong societies by telling our stories of resilience so that others can draw inspiration from them.

Part I
Dr. Jossine Abrahams

Dr. Jossine Abrahams is the founder and C.E.O. of Peace for Global Women. The website for the organisation is www.peaceforglobalwomen.com.

She is also the Africa chairperson for Ladies of All Nations International (LOANI), a grouping of women around the world who empower each other and aspire to change the world. Jossine is a philanthropist and an inspirational speaker. She runs her healthcare business and grocery shop in London. She also runs an authorship club called Aspiring Authors' Vision where she teaches people how to write books. She has authored sixteen books and this one will be her seventeenth book. Eight of the books are anthologies that she authored with people round the globe and some of her 'aspiring authors'.

Jossine enjoys working with women across the globe, especially those affected by domestic violence and abuse. She mentors them by way of motivation and works with them to change their situation to a better one. She believes in women's collaboration and encourages women to 'speak to heal' as being voiceless can cause physical and mental health problems. Her love of writing was prompted domestic violence and abuse that she experienced during the time of her marriage.

Jossine lives in London and she said the advantage of living in London is its diversity. She has worked with different charity organisations and the one she has done the most work with is Save the Children.

Jossine has travelled worldwide speaking at different places. For example, in Canada she has spoken on women in the workplace. In Florida, USA she spoke at the '100 Successful Women' event. She has travelled on speaking arrangements in India (New Delhi), USA (New York), Switzerland, New Zealand, Italy, South Africa and Zimbabwe. Jossine has helped many women in setting up businesses and assisted women to learn to be self employed by way of education and through encouraging them to set collaborative projects. She believes empowered women would do more than just get income to feed their children.

Jossine's experience as a health and social care lecturer allowed her to set up a care business in the United Kingdom.

Jossine is a recipient of many countless awards. She has Saviours' Award from LOANI, International Women Award from India, a BEFFTA (Black Entertainment Film Fashion Television Arts Sports

And Leadership) Award from London, a 100 Successful Women Award from the USA, a Speakers Award from London and Toronto, just to name a few. Jossine is one of the 50 most Inspiring women in the United Kingdom.

Jossine says that she is humbled by these achievements. She reminds people that God has blessed her so much and she strives to make this world a better place. She believes in women's collaboration. Her mantras are, 'Speak to Heal' and 'Together We Can'. Jossine hopes to touch as many lives as possible before she retires. She believes that every life matters and that every woman is a sister's keeper and she says that women are the best advocates for global growth and change.

Solo books by Jossine Abrahams

- *Curse or Blessing Being Spinster*
- *Challenges of a Living In Carer*
- *Peace After The Storm*
- *Freedom After Domestic Violence*
- *Empowered Women Speak Early*
- *Covid19 Speak to Heal*
- *The Hand of God: Testimony Maxwell Kabasa*

Anthologies by Jossine Abrahams

- *Depth of Her Soul*
- *Peace: A Perspective of Hope*
- *Vision Quest*

- *Bridled Strength*
- *The Innovative Leader*
- *The Effects of Covid19*
- *Untold Stories of Resilience*
- *Innovative Leadership, Volume 2*
- *Mending The Broken Hearted*
- *Closure of the Opened Wound*
- *Against All Odds: True stories about overcoming adversity and building resilience*

Chapter 1
What scared the hell out of me?

I was married three times. All the three men died of various causes. To face the future, I had to be strong. I was widowed three times. What a challenge in life for a young woman to be facing! I got married to my first husband at twenty-two years of age. A year later, I had a baby girl. The following year my husband was involved in a car accident and died on the spot. Heartbroken and challenged, I had to struggle to pick up the pieces and move on. I went for another two years as a single mother and then I met someone I loved.

The urge to get married again set in. I hated being single. I got married again at the age of twenty-six. My husband was a handsome man who worked as a teacher at a nearby primary school. I counted myself lucky because teaching was a respected profession. I thought I had won the jackpot. All was going well until he started to drink a lot. I noticed many things changing in my life and around me. Sometimes he came home late after work or he never came back. I often landed in serious trouble whenever I asked where he had been. We had many arguments and this became a constant occurrence. Each time I asked why he was not coming home, he would get very angry. I did not know the worst was to come.

When he was late home, I knew he would always be drunk and totally wasted. The man I loved turned into an abusive, arrogant alcoholic. He became a rapist and a wife beater. In a week, I could be raped several times. If I refused, I would be beaten up to the extent that I could not go to work. The physical bruises and swelling on my face did not bother him. Why would they? Sometimes he would beat me up and I would bleed and pass out on many occasions.

Many problems arose after. We both started missing work. He was always drunk and would miss work. I could not face my work colleagues because I had been beaten up badly. This carried on for over a year. The school authorities where he worked noticed that he turned up for work drunk. He was given several warnings, but he did not heed them. He was eventually fired. He dumped all his frustrations on me. The alcoholism continued and got worse. He was now drinking daily. He beat and raped me daily, accusing me of sleeping with everyone at work. It got so serious to the point of threatening me with a knife. That is when I decided, 'Enough is enough'. I had to tell someone in case the worst happened. On one occasion, I slept outside the house. He could not remember the reason why I did not sleep in our home.

My daughter was in boarding school and doing very well. However, I rarely saw her during the holidays, as she preferred to spend time with my father or my brothers. She could not see much of what was going on and what I was going through. In any case, I did not want to expose her to the abuse that I was facing. I was also afraid that she would be abused as I was.

I shared my plight with my friend and neighbour. She could not believe that my husband, who appeared to be a quiet man to everyone, could do that. She told the story to her husband who was a police officer. They called me into their house one afternoon and the husband took a statement from me. He assured me that he would come to rescue me if I ever am beaten up again. It was not a matter of if I am beaten up again, but when. The police officer gave me a small key ring that I had to press the next time my husband beat me up. The key ring would trigger an alarm in their house. We did not have to wait long. Before the end of that week my 'normal' routine of rape started. When I resisted the rape by pushing him away, he started beating me up. I remembered to press the key ring. The police officer next door came in and arrested my husband. The case was brought before the court and he was found guilty and sentenced to six months in prison.

I took his absence as an opportunity to get rid of him. I packed all his clothes and belongings and took them to his family. After serving his time, he was barred by the police from setting foot anywhere I lived or worked. I was happy to be a free woman again at the age of twenty-eight. This is how my second marriage collapsed, just like that.

I stayed single for another three years before loneliness kicked in again. This time I was rather desperate, thinking I was getting too old. I was feeling the pressure from family and church members and felt that society was judging me harshly.

At the age of thirty-three, I met another man, a divorcee with three children. I quickly jumped into marriage again because of pressure from society and because I felt that I was getting old. The first two years of marriage were great. However, things started to change in the third year. This man had a transport business. His trucks transported crops and grain from farms to the Grain Marketing Board in the capital city for processing. Like my previous husband, he started spending nights away from home on the pretext that he was working. When I asked why he was not spending nights at home, he would get annoyed and go away for a week or two. When he finally came home, he would infect me with all sorts of Sexually Transmitted Infections (STIs). I had endless trips to hospital for treatments. I had discomfort in my tummy, discharge from my private parts, and painful genital swelling. I knew this was not right and had to do something about it. The doctors gave me several warnings.

I later discovered that my husband was sleeping with several women, but it was rather too late. The women started harassing me and they would call the house phone looking for my husband. We had many arguments because of the women calling, but also because I was refusing to sleep with him. I had been warned by the doctors of the high risk of being infected and getting ill from STIs again. I was also being beaten up. On occasion, he would go out after beating me up to sleep at one of the girlfriends' house. I 'accepted' this behaviour as normal, again. I was fed up! However, I could not see a way out and I was worried at how family and friends would view me if I got divorced again.

Things got bad when one day I came back from work and noticed that he and the kids were gone. That was husband number three gone. I was alone again and afraid to face the world. Two months later, I heard that he had been admitted to an infectious diseases hospital. I went to see him, not because I loved or cared for him. I went to tell him that I was pregnant. When I saw him, he was nothing but skin and bones. He had become very skinny and dark. I could not recognize him. I took one glance at him and threw up. I could not even mention the purpose of my visit. I was shocked! Moreover, I was distraught. My friend held my hand and walked me out. After a while, I went back again to make sure it was really him not a ghost. I was even more confused and horrified.

I left the room where he was and went to ask the doctors what was wrong with him. The doctor nonchalantly replied, "AIDS!" "What?" I could not believe my ears. I was shocked and immediately felt sick. I was confused and could not make sense of anything. My mind was all over the place. I felt like a zombie and started to hallucinate in broad daylight.

After several days of pain and agony, my friend booked me an appointment to go and see a doctor. The appointment was for the following week. I lost the pregnancy due to stress. At the same time, I found that I was HIV positive. To add salt to the wound, I also discovered that my husband had passed away in hospital. It was very overwhelming to deal with the speed at which events were going.

I kept asking to myself, 'Now who can tell me how to handle this?'

'How on earth can I tell someone my story?' I pondered. 'Who would want to be near me if they knew what I have been through?'

During that time, the HIV/AIDS pandemic was rife. The stigma was unbearable. People were dying in large numbers. At the cemetery, funeral processions were given time slots, and there were queues of families waiting to bury their loved ones. I found myself lonely and suicidal. I wanted to kill myself to escape the shame and the pain. I was angry and frustrated. I could not understand what I had done wrong and why my life should be cut short because of love. There was no support system available. It was impossible to discuss my condition with my family. I was shaking daily. I completely lost my mind. Moreover, I was now dealing with my crisis secretly and that made the pain even worse. All I was thinking about constantly was, 'I am about to die' or 'I am paranoid' or 'I am stuffing food, so I am maintaining good weight'. The mirror became my best friend and my foe. I kept checking for changes in my figure. I did not want anyone to say that I was losing weight. I would tell myself, 'At least I'm fat, I am not losing weight.'

They say, 'Trouble comes in threes'. As I was going through all this pain, I received more bad news. My second husband has died due to alcohol poisoning. I now went into a severe depression. The pain was unbearable. If I had been thinking about killing myself, I was now seriously considering suicide as the only possible outlet left to get rid of the pain that I was experiencing. What would anyone do if they were in my situation?

By a stroke of luck I was fortunate meet someone I prefer to call a 'Good Samaritan'. This person took me overseas to Britain where I started to live again. I got access to medication, and became mentally and physically fit and strong. My confidence and self-esteem came back. I started a new chapter in my life, away from the pain and trauma that I had experienced in my country of birth. I felt the urge to help other people who were in my position but not able to get out of their dire situation. I thought my life struggles would inspire them to realise that there is always light at the end of the tunnel. I started writing books as an escape route from my troubles. I wanted to help women who were victims of domestic violence and sexual exploitation. I trained and qualified to lecture in colleges. I am now an author. I also motivate and encourage women to speak up about all forms of abuse. I help women to reinvent their lives and encourage them to seek help when they are in toxic relationships.

I thank God for the opportunity to be able to know Him, get help from church, and hospital with the incredible staff, doctors, nurses, and counselors. I am happy. I have lived for 30 years after my diagnosis. Had I killed myself when I felt suicidal, would I be here helping other women? I am glad I found favour upon my life. I made the right decision to forgive those who put scars in my life. I am a grandmother. I love life. My mission is not finished until God calls me. Be strong dear reader, dear friend. Do not take your life. Believe in God. He has plans for you and me. My HIV diagnosis was only a scar. For over fifteen years, the HIV virus in my system is not detectable. It is not there. I attribute this to my inner strength to bounce back.

Resilience!

Chapter 2
Peace after the storm

"A Psalm of David. The Lord is my shepherd; I shall not want. He makes me lie down in green pastures. He leads me beside still waters. He restores my soul. He leads me in paths of righteousness for his name's sake. Even though I walk through the valley of the shadow of death, I will fear no evil, for you are with me; your rod and your staff, they comfort me. You prepare a table before me in the presence of my enemies; you anoint my head with oil; my cup overflows. ..."

Psalm 23, Verse 1-6

One has to make a choice and draw the line. Do you want to hurt all your life or you want to live a good life? After those good thirty years of emotionally pressurising my heart and my brain, I had to make a strong decision to die or not to die.

I then found it worthy to start healing to release myself from anger, hurt and deceit. I fought this war in silence, but I finally decided it was time to educate others and save lives. I felt that if I saved even just one life, I would have achieved my goal. I felt that if I did not do this, my people would die of lack of knowledge. If I was not going to help, my suffering and my pain would not have been worthy of anything.

I vowed not to be like my parents who believed in keeping abusive relationships a secret because they had received *lobola*. Those aunts and uncles who married me away had benefited by getting some money and they were determined to make sure that I stayed in the marriage, despite all the abuse that I got from it.

This culture of being 'everyone's child' should be abolished. I understand the idea that it takes a community to raise a child. Nevertheless, that maxim is not tantamount to abuse and infliction of pain on the child that is being raised. It is not a ticket to torment young women. Having a group of villagers decide on my life at my expense seems like a harsh and cruel act. It defeats the whole purpose of raising a child in a community where individuals and morals are respected.

Hope and prayer kept me going during my storm. In silence, I would cry myself a river and sleep. I turned my pillow when the tears had soaked one side of it. I cried myself to sleep so that I could keep my marriage alive and for fear of being an outcast. Was there any marriage or love or was I was only a piece of meat?

I thank you Lord for the good years I struggled in turmoil. It was because of my ordeal that I became a resilient and strong woman. My experience from those tribulations keeps me optimistic and hoping for a better tomorrow. It lifted the heavy load that was on my shoulders.

My goal is to set myself free for generations to come. By speaking and writing about my experience of domestic violence and domestic abuse, I hope to save many people. I liberated myself and the pain will never hound me again. However, that is just part of the story. I now need to focus on others who may not be as lucky as I was to come out of such a situation.

I chose to be an author of domestic violence stories to save lives, not just from domestic violence and abuse, but also from HIV and AIDS. Contracting HIV during the storm will always be a reminder of the struggle and pain that I went through and that memory will remain with me until I die. Although my CD4 count is high and my viral load is undetectable, there are moments of weakness and of sickness which make me uncomfortable. I have to always remember that my immune system is not strong and could easily be compromised. I should keep myself active and well.

Taking pills everyday has become part of my life. However, taking them for thirty years has had its own impact on me. I ask myself always, "Am I normal or not?" I convince myself, "Yes I am normal." Tablets slow down my energy levels some times and some days are unbearable, but I am resilient.

Chapter 3
No stone unturned

As we all know when the storm comes, it leaves no stone unturned. The ground shakes and the trees are left without leaves. Some of the houses were moved to different locations and some were destroyed and vanished. I had to be like a lion in its den and stood up to face the storm. What a challenge to my life!

God made sure he kept me alive so I can testify to the world. Who am I to say it just happened? I am not cleverer than everyone else is. The favour of God kept me going. Looking back, I have now come to believe that maybe the HIV diagnosis was a scare that made me realise that I was in an abusive relationship. An important event stopped me from sleepwalking into another marriage. I was freed to do the work that I am doing now. There is nothing wrong, after all, in staying single. Being a single woman has so many advantages. I can do this important work without anyone making me feel worthless. Culture or no culture, I am still standing. I am happy. I am healthy. I am using my pain to inspire others.

While I realise the importance of cultural norms and practices, like those that accompany *lobola* payments, I also feel that they constrict progress. They perpetuate behaviours that promote abuse and exploitation of women and the girl child. I feel that these cultural practices are not right. They do not promote independence, creativity, love and family cohesion. In fact, they do the opposite. They promote family problems and are divisive. There is no love if love is based on commodification of women.

Traditionally and even today, *lobola* money in many families is taken to educate male members of the family and fund their leisure moments. Yet lobola was meant to promote family cohesion, family ties and family progress. It was meant to bring two families together in a spirit of love, respect and understanding.

People may argue that this is Africa, and Africa has its own practices. That may be true, but human rights are indivisible. They are universal and all societies should be involved in their pursuit. While lobola traditionally was a way of making money, there are other means of living and there are other ways of making money.

I would never hurt my parents. Cultural practices put pressure on them. I think they could have thought about me as well. I guess my father could not do it alone, as I mentioned before.

In Africa, I am not only my father's daughter, but a daughter of the whole village. They say it takes a village to raise a child. It took a village to demand *lobola* too. As for my mother, I am sure she was inwardly hurting too. She had no voice as not all women had a voice in such matters.

The situation now seems to be changing since the growing calls for the emancipation of women. Many changes have taken place in my native Zimbabwe since the early 1980s. I hope and pray that these changes will keep coming so that the value of a woman is recognised and respected. It is my sincere hope that these change brought in society will allow women not to be seen as chattels like pieces of furniture that are only there to decorate the household.

With God, all things are possible. I now understand my purpose in life much better. I also understand that I can be happy being single, but also that I am capable of forming good and lasting relationships. I have found a way to protect myself inwardly and outwardly. I can confront whatever comes my way. I do not lose sleep over some of the things I used to worry about anymore.

I find comfort in the Bible and knowing who I am before Christ. He has given me my life back. Now I do not have nightmares of my future. I am excited about the future. Even though I do not have any physical relationship with anyone, I have a spiritual relationship with my father, Jesus Christ. I do not fear anything or anyone. I am a fighter and I fight a good fight. I receive anything that comes my way and I allow my Father to give me strength to win that fight.

Temptation is always there, but the power of God restrains me from getting involved in things that could lead me back to where I am coming from. Thank you Lord. My life has shifted to the best side. I count myself lucky. My role now is to counsel young girls about life. I am a Life Coach and I have the love of life.

If I trace my life journey and the storm that I encountered along the way, I can safely say God saved me for a reason. I still have the support of my family. My father is still alive. Thank God for his life. He is in his mid-80s now. He too has transformed and understood some of the pressures that culture and society imposed on the family. He also found God and he is a devout Christian. He is also a blessing to my children.

I never remarried after all I went through. I never had any more children after my one and only child. My God has been so faithful to me. My daughter now has two girls of her own, my grandchildren whom I have adopted as mine. I am a blessed grandmother and I love life. They say, "Make hay while the sun shines." Until the day I die, I will continue to serve young men and women and save lives.

Part 2
Elizabeth Saji

Chapter 4
Soar on wings like an Eagle...
against all odds

On a cold November night at four minutes past eight, I gave birth to a healthy bouncing baby boy. It was a defining moment, one that transformed my life in so many ways. I felt honoured by God to have been given the opportunity to take part in creating another human being. I was blessed! I was fortunate enough to have a short labour and an easy straightforward delivery, which was a great start to my journey to motherhood.

However, my life has not always been that easy and straightforward. Just six months prior to the birth of my son, I had gone through some of the darkest days of my life. The father of my son walked out on me on the eve of our first wedding anniversary. I was eleven weeks pregnant, blooming and looking forward to married life with a new baby on the way.

It was springtime in May. The weather was lovely and the sun was shining. On this particular day, my husband woke up in a very good mood. We danced away to some Shona music while we prepared to go out for the day. He was a funny man who made me laugh and I enjoyed his company. Earlier that morning, he had given me some money to get my hair braided so 'I would look nice for church the following day'. Little did I know that he just needed time to pack his bags and leave me.

We left the house and went our separate ways as he was going to get a haircut at a different place, but unbeknown to me, that would be the last time I would see him. I called him a few hours later to tell him my hair was beautifully done and I was looking forward to seeing the smile on his face. He seemed 'a bit off' on the phone and sounded like he was distracted. He said he would see me later.

When I did not hear back from him, I called again but he had switched off his phone, so I became worried that something had happened to him. I hurried home to find out, but I walked into an empty flat that looked like it had been burgled. The door had been left unlocked. The cupboard doors were open and there were things scattered everywhere. I remembered leaving the place looking nice and tidy earlier that morning, but now it looked a mess. I later found out that my husband had returned home, hurriedly packed his bags and left without saying goodbye. He did not even leave a note!

My world came crashing down, I felt rejected, hurt and heartbroken. My eyes were filled with darkness, and I felt numb and confused. Somehow, in my spirit, I immediately knew this was it and that although I had not been given any warning whatsoever, my marriage was finished.

'*But why this way though?*' my spirit asked God.

It felt so surreal.

I was so broken that I could not even cry, so I just sat on the floor feeling lifeless. I desperately wished he could have at least started a fight or just some silly argument so that I could have been mad at him. Maybe I could have handled his walking away better.

I felt crushed and wished the ground would just open up and swallow me. At the same time, there were loads of thoughts racing through my mind and I remembered lots of Bible verses including my favourite one, Jeremiah 29 v 11. It reads, "*For I know the thoughts and plans that I have for you, declares the Lord, thoughts and plans to prosper you and not to harm you, plans to give you hope and a future.*"

I felt overwhelmed and more confused whilst my mind wondered, '*what kind of a God allows this?*' What does He even mean saying '*plans to prosper me and not harm me*' and then make me go through this pain?

I wanted to scream badly, but also did not want to attract the attention of my neighbours, so I suppressed the urge. I eventually calmed down and felt more sober. I paced up and down the flat and spoke calmly to God. I would not even call it praying because I was just speaking out and making closed sentences.

I was angry and told God that since He had allowed this to happen to me, He left me no choice, but to totally surrender myself to Him and be His full responsibility. This was not part of my plan, but it sure looked like it was part of His plan. I had no choice but to be at His mercy. I therefore decided to trust Him and allow Him to go before me.

"The Lord Himself goes before you: He will be with you. He will never leave you nor forsake you. Do not be afraid or discouraged." (Deuteronomy 31 v 8).

But the physical man in me was hurting and still needed physical and emotional healing, so I allowed myself time to wallow in misery for a few weeks before wiping my tears and shaking off the dust. I then made the decision to concentrate on my pregnancy and focus on the health of both my baby and I. Even though it proved challenging, I soaked myself in the word of God and put my hope in Him.

'Those whose hope is in the Lord will renew their strength. They will soar on wings like eagles; they will run and not grow weary, they will walk and not be faint'. (Isaiah 40 v 31)
God was faithful and in good time, I found my strength. I felt fit enough to return to work and made arrangements to move in with my sister so I had support during my pregnancy.

I am a believer of the gospel of Jesus Christ and I consider myself Christian. I was born again when I was 15 years old and in high school. Although I now attend a Pentecostal church, I was raised Catholic and was taught to believe the word of God from a very young age. However, sometimes it takes a very painful experience to fully understand and believe what the bible says.

Through the mess of my rejection and pain, God gave me a wonderful message and opened my eyes to the wonders of His word. I began to see myself as an eagle like the bible says and I took time to study the life of eagles.

'The eagle is the only bird that actually loves the challenges brought by a storm. Whilst other birds will fly away, eagles fearlessly fly into fierce winds, using the storm current to rise higher in a matter of seconds. The pressure of the storm helps them to glide without using their energy as their wings' unique design allows them to lock in a fixed position amid violent storm winds' according to Atlanta Journal-Constitution online (ACJ.com).

The direction of my life totally changed after my husband left. I had no script for the new life I was about to face and this was not the future I had imagined for myself. It felt like I was facing a big wild storm and God gently reminded me of His word in Isaiah 40 v 31. I had to believe His word and be like an eagle in order to face that storm before me.

I needed to trust that God had *'plans to prosper me and not harm me'* and that *'He would go before me and be with me'*. Therefore, like an eagle I prepared to fearlessly fly into the storm and soar to great heights. However, before I could fly, I had to learn to do so, and just as a mother eagle stirs up its nest, God made my life uncomfortable so I could test my wings and learn to fly. The experience was tough, but God patiently hovered over me for protection and spread His wings ready to catch me.

'As an eagle stirs up its nest and hovers over its young, He spreads His wings to catch them on His pinions' (Deuteronomy 32 v 11).

'Spiritually the eagle can signify inspiration and release from bondage and victory' (ACJ.com). When my husband left, what followed was a series of great defining moments. Even though they felt painful and heart breaking, I believe the experiences were my release from bondage to victory.

Whilst marriage is of God and honourable in his sight, *"Therefore a man shall leave his father and his mother and hold fast to his wife and they shall become one flesh"* (Genesis 2 v 24).

My experience was one of rejection and pain and this is my story!

Chapter 5
Great sense of resilience

The more I likened myself to an eagle, the stronger I felt within and I developed a great sense of resilience about my situation. I waited until I felt cheerful and confident enough to own my story before I gathered the strength to face the world again.

I soon began going out to social gatherings and meeting people again although it was very challenging to stay positive after telling people that '*I am pregnant and oh by the way, the father of the baby left*'. I received a mixture of responses, whilst some people genuinely felt sorry for me and gladly offered their support; some people were just plain insensitive and passed hurtful remarks. However, I survived and faced my storm as an eagle. I had prepared myself and built up my confidence in the presence of God before coming out. I had felt an unworthy, rejected and unlovable woman to one mortal man yet to God Himself, I was '*fearfully and wonderfully made*'. So I held on to the promises of God:

"*Since you are precious and honoured in my sight, and because I love you, I will give men in exchange for you and people in exchange for your life*" (Isaiah 43 v 4).

I chose to define myself according to the word of God and took charge of writing the next chapter of my life. I took time to pamper myself and whispered '*I love you!*' each time I looked in the mirror. I looked forward to my antenatal classes, even though I sometimes ended up feeling sad when the other women talked about their husbands and partners.

I had always wanted a son so whilst I was in a good place, I decided it was time to start talking to God about my baby's gender. By this time, I had spent so much time in prayer; I felt so close to God and fully trusted Him. We had such long deep conversations and I was confident that He had granted my request for a son. Before my husband left, we had started listing possible names for the baby as a couple, so I had an idea of what name I wanted. However, after specifically asking God for a 'man child' like Hannah, I was grateful that He had answered my prayer so I decided to name him Samuel.

"So in the course of time Hannah conceived and gave birth to a son. She named him Samuel, saying 'Because I asked the Lord for him' " (I Samuel I v 20).

By the time I went for my ultrasound scan, I was certain it was a boy and I was overjoyed when it was actually confirmed by the scan. The joy of carrying that baby boy helped me numb the pain of my heartbreak and I was over the moon. I am the eldest of four girls and growing up, I had watched my parents long for a son, so I had started praying for my own as a young girl. Hence now that I was finally going to give birth to my very own son, I was overwhelmed with joy and marvelled in the grace of God. However, I still had some bad days when I felt emotionally low and remembered my heartbreak, but I survived against all odds and thrived physically, facing the storm like an eagle.

I had moved in with my sister during my pregnancy and had managed to save up a bit of money and I had the opportunity to put my finances in order. Consequently, I managed to get a decent mortgage and bought myself a nice flat in order to start a new life with my baby. By the grace of God, I remained in very good physical health throughout the pregnancy and delivered a healthy bouncing baby boy.

The birth of my son was one of the best experiences of my life; I became a 'creator'. God was gracious enough to give me the privilege of becoming a mother and I did not take that lightly. Still I could not help being sad that I would be raising him on my own. I had already started divorce proceedings and I knew there was no hope for reconciliation. This next challenge was to be my biggest storm yet, divorced single mother raising a boy. But God is faithful. He promised to 'never leave me nor forsake me'. Where I come from, we have the saying: 'Mwari havadhakwe', meaning God never gets drunk. He is always sober. Therefore, I trusted that He was fully aware of my situation.

"Whoever dwells in the shelter of the Most High will rest in the shadow of the Almighty. I will say of the Lord, "He is

my refuge and my fortress, my God in whom I trust"
(Psalms 91 v 1-2).

I had planned to give my son the middle name 'Munana' (which means miracle in my native language), but as soon I saw his cute little face, I decided I needed more than one miracle every day to raise him on my own so I named him 'Minana', which is plural for miracles. It felt so surreal, but this time in a good way, I was so happy to finally become a mum, I felt the peace of God. Once again, I chose to trust Him as I flew straight into the next big storm of my life as a single parent.

In my culture, once you become a parent, you are addressed by your first child's name so I embraced that honour and became 'Mai Sammy' (Samuel's mum). My identity changed and I loved the change. To this day, I still feel tickled when I get called 'Mai Sammy', it is such a wonderful feeling and I love it! Being a single parent definitely comes with its pros and cons, 'it's twice the work, twice the stress, twice the tears but twice the hugs, twice the love and twice the pride'.

I started the year 2009 on a high, new baby, new title (Mai Sammy) and the icing on the cake, a brand new home! The beginning was rough though, trying to adjust to life as a new mum, going without sleep and not having the other parent's help or support. Luckily I was surrounded by loving family and friends who were always there to support me with child care. I was always rushing around, feeling stressed, anxious or overwhelmed and sometimes even confused.

However, I soon discovered that I actually got a thrill from the rushing around and thoroughly enjoyed it all. My baby boy gave me so much joy, it felt (and still feels) like I have sunshine every day. I became so used to thriving on the adrenaline caused by the stress such that, as soon as my life calmed down, I became restless and looked for something else to be anxious about.

However with time, my journey became even more challenging and sometimes more painful but I also had times of great fun and excitement. With each new challenge, came a new opportunity to test my faith in God. I learned to constantly remind myself of my status as an eagle and that God is constantly watching over me, protecting me and ready to catch me as I continued to fly right into the storms of my life: Deuteronomy 32 v 11.

Following six months of maternity leave, I returned to work when Sammy was about seven months old. Although I worked part-time, it always felt like over-time, I was so tired but there was no break from my mum job. I earned a lot less money working part-time but it was worth it because I got to spend precious time with my son. I was always exhausted and sometimes I did not even know what day of the week it was. Nevertheless, I got so used to the fast-paced exhausting lifestyle possibly due to maternal instincts and I flourished as a mum.

When Sammy was about three years old, I decided to go back to studying and upgrade myself. I had qualified as a General Nurse with a Diploma of Higher Education a few years earlier. I approached my boss and asked for the opportunity to study towards a bachelor's degree. God was gracious and I was granted the funding and paid time off to undertake the studies. It was a tough ride, but I had become so used to thriving on adrenaline. I thoroughly enjoyed the challenge and I went on to graduate with a First Class Bachelor's degree in Health Care Practice. I did so well, I was also awarded the St George's University London, Kathy McGovern prize for 'most outstanding performance' by a Continuing Professional Development student.

The eagle in me continued to soar and after that, I was awarded a fully funded National Institute of Health Research (NIHR) studentship to do a Master's degree full time. By the time Samuel turned six years old, I had completed my second degree and I graduated with a Masters in Clinical Research (MRes) with distinction.

I went back to work full time and I have been slowly working my way up the professional ladder. I say 'slowly because I consider myself to be a full-time mum first, which is currently a 24-hour job. My profession is a second job.

Samuel continues to give me so much joy. He is a wonderful kid; loving, kind and considerate. He is very smart, talented and creative. He recently started high school and is doing very well. Because of him, I see all my struggles and pain as gifts which have allowed me to be strong, resilient, tenacious and passionate about doing well.

My struggles have also taught me to be compassionate towards others who have gone through similar pain and struggles. I know the feeling of rejection firsthand and I can relate.

Samuel's father chose not to be involved in his life, but God Himself is 'a *father to the fatherless*'. This is painful and challenging to accept, but I continue to trust in God to fight my battles and '*stand in the gap*' for my son. *He said, "Listen, King Jehoshaphat and all who live in Judah and Jerusalem! This is what the Lord says to you: 'Do not be afraid or discouraged because of this vast army. For the battle is not yours, but God's"* (2 Chronicles 20 v 15).

'*He saw that there was no one, He was appalled that there was no one to intervene; therefore His own arm brought salvation to Him, and His own righteousness sustained Him*' (Isaiah 59 v 16).

Twelve years on, my mess has become my message. As I continue on my journey as a single parent, I continue to grow and soar to great heights like the eagle I was created to be. Every day is a new opportunity for me to face yet another wild storm and soar even higher.

Going forward, I will not settle for anything less than God's best for me!

Part 3
Nyasha Muradzikwa

Chapter 6
Lost everything and got back more

For six years, I owned a nursing agency in South East London. Business was good. I was making good money and riding the wave of the health and social care boom. My plan was to ride the business all the way to retirement. Everything I was reading from the health and social car journals and just the news, in general, all said the same thing. That for the next 20 years healthcare was going to be a boom, because we live in an aging society. Therefore, I figured I was set. My plan was to retire in 15 years. The boom was going to last forever, so I had nothing to worry about.

All of a sudden, I got hit with the sucker punch in 2007-2008 when the world financial crisis hit. We all know what happened then. I went from getting four to five contracts a month to doing two or three contracts a year. Needless to say, my finances went right down the tubes, but my plan was to keep the business going until the market came back. That was my plan anyway. I did what I needed to do to keep the business afloat. I had money put aside that I was using to keep my head above water.

I was squeaking along trying to hold everything together when I got hit with the second sucker punch, a Care Quality Commission de-registration, and that was when the commission in its infinite wisdom decided to put a ton more regulation on top of the ton of regulation that was already in place. I had not complied.

With that, the little girl from Zimbabwe just could not survive, so that was the final nail in the coffin. I and the two people who worked for me, were left out in the cold. Since I was self-employed, I had no solid bank history to find a personal loan to save my business. What made matters worse I had used all my money trying to keep the business going, so I could no longer pay the rent. I was evicted from my apartment. What made matters worse was that I had my car repossessed. So there I was 50 years old, no place to live, no business, no job, no income, and no money; nothing. It was not exactly the high point of my life.

What did I do? What would you do?

Well, I did something I never thought I would do and really did not want to do, but I was left with little choice. I put my tail between my legs and called my ex-husband. (How humiliating do you think that was?) I was lucky that we were always on friendly terms so he said I could stay with him until I got back on my feet. He would never admit this, but it worked out pretty good for him as well. At that point, I became like a live-in maid. I made sure dinner was on the table when he got home. I kept the house neat and did the chores that needed to be done. You can see he made out alright, but like I said, he would never admit it.

There I was sitting in my x-husband's house, and I started to do the things I needed to do to develop an income. I started to call old contacts to see if there was anything happening in the industry. I was on all the job search sites and sent out a ton of CVs. I did all this and got back a lot of nothing. So it did not take me long to realise that it might be because of my age. I faced the fact that at my age not too many people are beating down the door to hire me, so I decided I had to do something on my own to generate an income.

I knew I had to stay productive. I did not want to get caught up in a routine that so many unemployed people do when they are out of work for a long period of time. They get up, turn on the T.V. and that is it. That is all they do for the rest of the day. I did not want to get caught up in that, so at 9am the T.V. went off and I jumped on the computer to do my searches. I have to admit: half the time I did not know what I was searching for, but I had to stay productive. I just want to bring up a point.

You would think because I had the healthcare business that I was at least great on the computer. This could not be farther from the truth. At that point, the only things I knew how to do on the computer was to fill out a loan application, print it, send e-mails and search for beauty products on

Amazon. That was the extent of my knowledge on the computer.

On one of my daily searches I ran across this header that caught my eye, it said *The Secret, How To Attract Wealth*. Being in the situation I was in, it drew me in like a magnet, so I clicked on it and it turned out to be an old Oprah show. She had a guest who was explaining how we all have the ability to attract wealth as long as we do certain things a certain way.

I think I read it about five or six times and I said to myself this makes sense, a lot of sense. I called my sister and asked her for a couple of hundred pounds so I could invest in the system, which I did. After a while, I was amazed at how much better I started to feel. My confidence level started to come back. I started thinking clearer and was more focused and for the first time in a while, I started to realise that my future was not as black as I once thought it was.

Now that I was facing things with a positive attitude, I knew I had to take control of my life and generate my income because I was getting nowhere with my job searches. And I was not about to go to work at McDonald's and have some 17-year-old snot nose manager tell me how to fry some burgers. Since I was sitting at home and had the computer, some kind of home-based business was the only thing I could do. I started to do my research.

I found out that there are over two billion dollars spent online every year and it is expected to double within five years. Now that is a lot of money. I said to myself I need to get in on the action. I was not looking to be Richard Branson or Alan Sugar, I just wanted to be sliced up to make £50,000-£60,000 and I was alright with that.

So I jumped in headfirst and put all my efforts into starting an Internet business. At this time, I knew nothing about how to navigate around the computer, and it turned out to be the most frustrating and aggravating time in my life. Now I know the true meaning of the saying, "you can't teach an old dog new tricks." It was really hard, but because I was thinking about the positive side of things and was focused I stuck with it.

Although I have to admit there were days I wanted to put my fist through the monitor, remember I was sitting on that computer between 6 – 9 hours a day so sometimes it got to me.

I got to the point where I figured that I knew enough to put up my first website. It took me four days to put it up – which is really a long time considering how it now takes me half an hour to put one together. But I was proud as I could be, remember I went from not knowing anything about the computer to putting up a website. I will be honest with you here. As I look back, it was not very good, but at the time, I was proud as I could be. After a little more trial and error and some tweaking, it was ready to be published on-line.

After a short time, I received my first payment for a grand total of £34. This is not a typo £34. Most people might have thrown in the towel after eight months had gone by and all I had to show for eight months of aggravation and frustration was an income of £34. But I was thinking on the positive side of things and was really focused so that £34 actually got me excited.

I remember thinking wow you can really make money at this and it gave me the incentive to keep going. I remember thinking if I can make £34 I can make £334. I remember when my ex-husband got home that night I showed him the payment. He looked at me and then looked at the payment again. He then looked at me and said: "You're never getting out of here are you?"

I have to give him credit that was the first time in all those months he ever said anything. However, I was focused, so I kept going. Soon after that, I received a 375 payment, then a £125 payment, then £200. £200 does not sound like a lot of money, but you have to remember for all those months, I was totally broke. I really mean dead broke so to all of a sudden have £200 I was on cloud nine.

So now, I had money coming in. I set up another care agency, but now backed up by money that I was making from my online businesses. Today I employ more than 50 carers and 20 nurses.

I had a positive mental attitude and things were looking good, that is until I looked in the mirror. After months of just sitting in front of the computer, I had put on 20 kilogrammes. I immediately went on a very strict diet of nothing, but salads. I also knew I had to start exercising.

Although I had money coming in, I did not feel I was making enough at that point to pay for gym membership. Overall, those months of having no money, it is easy to become cheap. You know cheap is a harsh word, let us call it being frugal. Anyway, I was self-conscious about my appearance and I did not want to be seen by anyone. I went over to Homebase to find something I could use at home. As I was walking up the aisle, an exercise ball caught my eye. Well, let me be honest here. It was not the exercise ball, but the price tag under it. Remember I was frugal. It was the price tag of £15 that caught my eye. The ball just happened to be above it. So I bought it and took it home.

When I got the exercise ball home, I developed a routine of my own. I called the routine Over 50 And Having A Ball, a play on words. I used it for half an hour in the morning and half an hour at night.

At this point, things could not be going better. I had three websites up generating income every month, I had a positive attitude about everything (even my ex-husband) and the weight was coming off. After a long time, life was good again.

At this time I was also following a fitness blog and me and the owner of the blog were e-mailing each other.

He told me his story, I told him mine. One day he e-mailed me and said I should think about writing my story because there are so many people out there in the same situation that I was in and that I might inspire and motivate some to take their lives back. After I thought about it for a while, I thought it was a good idea. That is when I got the idea to find Zimbabweans who were publishing and writing and I came across Dean Thompson Publishing. The rest is history. I now enjoy being an author, public speaker, and trainer.

*As a happy side note, after I moved in with my ex-husband, we realised that we still loved each other and we have been together ever since. You never know how life is going to turn out.

Now life has taken me in a new direction. I now show people how to stay happy and healthy in their Golden Years. It is never too late to start.

Chapter 7
Persistence and resilience

I am writing my story, in the hope that it will inspire you to realise your ability to use what is to create what can be in your life, your work and your world. The deepest questions, insights, awareness and answers rarely come when we are sitting at the top of the mountain of success feeling like the keys to the kingdom are in our right hand. No matter who we are, no matter what we have acquired and accomplished; our success, satisfaction, sense of personal power, value and fulfilment can change in a blink. I know because that is what happened to me.

My greatest challenge and greatest life, leadership and success lesson, as you read above, began when I was well after my 50th birthday. I was thrust from the mountain of success into a very dark valley. My age represented a giant fork or rut in the road of my personal life and career. It was a time when the gold I had created by the sweat of my brow had turned to dust. I had not done anything to justify what had occurred. It was a global financial crisis that has dealt me a huge blow.

I landed far, far, away from my former success as owner of a successful health and social care organisation, and the accouterments of success I had taken for granted. I faced a life crucible, an event of nightmarish proportion and that took me from the mountain of success to ground zero where I had to start my life and my career again. While I had overcome incredible hurdles building a formidable career, the hurdles that I faced after my 50th birthday took me to the abyss where survival itself was in question.

I spent time in a dark valley that was my greatest challenge and my greatest teacher.
I did not tell you that I had taken one of the most menial of jobs soon after the business folded—cleaning toilets. A life crucible, a crime, a tragedy had thrown me from the mountain of success to a very dark valley. On one of the days, I had £5 in my pocket, hoping that I would be able to recover enough money to start life again. I stood there, mop in hand, vowing to prove that with faith, courage, integrity one could transform even the greatest darkness into the greatest light.

Why is my story important? Because, being smart, fast, and well trained are no longer enough. The changes, challenges, and the crisis of uncertainty we face demand a different way of thinking, leading and living that can help us inspire, engage and lead the best in ourselves and others when the going is very tough…and even when the tough are not sure how to get going!

It was at ground zero, doing the most menial of jobs that I learned a secret, a truth, a lesson that changed my life. Inevitably, whether by old age or a twist of fate…all the glitters is never gold. The greatest power we hold is not in what we have, but in who we truly are when we choose to ignite, engage and unleash the leader or hero within. Our greatest power lies in our ability to use what is to create what can be in our self, our lives, our relationships, our leadership and our work.

The worst life crucible; the cruellest of treatment, abuse, humiliation, the greatest of failures, the pain of dealing with a threatening illness, or a personal stumbling block cannot steal the faith, hope, courage, potential and determination that burns inside us unless we let it. Things that will be irrelevant when we leave this earth cannot measure the greatest success we can ever achieve. Rather it will be measured by our ability to live, lead and succeed to purpose. It is our ability to live, lead and succeed to purpose, our ability to truly self-actualise by unleashing our true potential that can move molehills and mountains in our life and in the lives of others.

It is this purpose, this passion and this potential that creates value for others. Creating value for others is the timeless formula for success and fulfilment.

It is our ability to see past what is and create or re-create what can be that determines our ability to drive our greatest intentions forward, and reclaim our ability to live, lead and succeed to purpose.

For when we are on purpose, we also discover our joy factor. When we are on purpose there is a sense of profound happiness, fulfilment meaning, and empowerment that helps us unleash our best thoughts, emotions, and actions. The pilot light that connects us with our highest power and our greatest potential, the candle that can help us heal, restore and rebuild a life, a career, an organisation can be found and it can be re-engaged and re-ignited.

My story demonstrates that it was in the valley, at a time when all seemed lost, that I discovered my greatest power-my edge to create websites, sell products and make money. It was in the valley that I learned to love and accept myself for who I was, rather than measuring my worth by what I had acquired or accomplished. It was in the valley that I discovered how to use my strengths, stressors, changes and deepest challenges to build my greatest advantage and potential.

I learned to optimise my strength and skills while transforming the very difficult and gut wrenching challenges, challenges and crises I faced into breakthrough results that accelerated and sustained my so-called 3Q Strengths: My IQ (mind power-whole brain thinking, greater focus, quicker ideation, creativity, action-ability), EQ (emotional intelligence-emotional management and mastery) and SQ (spiritual quotient-the power within). Today, I have dedicated my life to helping others build their edge because I believe in the power of human being better, not simply living and doing faster.

Each human being has a special contribution to make; no matter how large or small, every contribution counts now more than ever before. Our greatest strength, success, and satisfaction cannot be sustained by what we command, control or acquire, but from what we contribute. It is the relationships that we build and sustain, our ability to inspire, engage and lead the best in ourselves that will take us forward.

Seize your ability to make a difference, because YOU can. I seized mine, started developing websites, selling products, motivating others and I think this is not bad for a plus-50 something woman from Zimbabwe.

Part 4
Tendai Chirima

Chapter 8
Married to a control freak

When I was married he liked to control everything, he thought it was what husbands were allowed to do...I felt I was a prisoner in my own home. I felt like a dog on a chain and I couldn't get off it'.

I was married and I was unhappy. He was violent and did not treat me right and he did not treat my family right either. He got nasty and nastier. Every day things just got worse.

When things got pretty bad, I managed and coped day by day by trying to ignore him. I would do my own thing at home trying to ignore him. If he started nagging at me or whatever, I would get in the car and go for a drive or go visit my mother's place or friends – just to get away from him. When I got back home, he would be sweet for a while then he would be back to the old nasty person.

When we were together, he was very strict about who I went out with. I could not easily go out with other people, girls or guys. I had no life. I felt I was a prisoner in my own home. If I did go out, it was only with my family or him. I felt like a dog on a chain and I could not get off it. When he went out to play his sport, I would sit up and wait for him as wives and husbands do for each other. Half the time he would come home and say, 'Why are you up?' I would think to myself, 'I'm just doing what couples do for each other'.

He hid money from me. I often thought where half our money had gone and it was hidden in his shed. I thought that is not on. He spent money on what he wanted, but I was not allowed. He would hide money, then spend money on stuff that he did not need, he would later say, 'I don't know why I bought that'. We were always broke. I told my family how it was in the marriage, but I did not tell his family. They would have just been on his side.

How things changed

I work at a business service for people with disabilities and they sent me to a relationship centre for counselling. I went to the service and they gave me a pamphlet about the local domestic violence outreach service. It was helpful to have information.

I spoke to my family about how I was feeling. I have a good relationship with my mother, father and sisters. I discussed with my family the information I found in the pamphlet, then with their support I decided to ring the number for the domestic violence outreach service that was on it.

Speaking to the staff at the outreach service was most helpful. They gave me good advice and I would not have been able to go through all of this without them. They supported my parents and me.

I decided I would I tell my husband to get out the door. I had my other, father and one of my sisters with me when I told him to go. Mum and dad told him he should go home to his parents' house for a while.

After I kicked him out, he kept coming around all the time and his attitude just kept getting worse and worse. I told him he had a lot of growing up to do. He said the same to me. He would call me a lot of horrible names, which I will not repeat, it was not very nice. In the end, I ended up calling him a few awful names myself. I got so angry.

We worked in the same place, which made it very difficult. It felt as if he would never leave me alone. It felt as if he was stalking me still, which he was. He was watching me, watching who I was with, people that I know at work, who I talked to.

Going to court

I had trouble getting an Intervention Order. I got one in the end, which is still current, but it did not make much difference anyway, he still did what he wanted. He just would not listen. He did what he wanted. He broke the Intervention Order a number of times; and still came down my street.

I would report it and we would go back to court, but it felt as if we were just wasting our time and nothing was happening. He is a liar; he lied and lied all the way through. Even the police knew he lied; he just lied and lied. He just lied all the time and I thought, 'How can you lie to the police.' But he did.

He harassed my mum and dad. He would ring them all hours of the day and night, especially when he was drunk and disruptive. One night he rang them seven times. It was unreal. I changed my telephone number to a private number so he could not reach me.

One day he stalked me in his car. I was driving along in my car and he drove up behind me and kept driving his car really close. It was dangerous and scary. That incident had to go back to court. They went right through him, but he kept denying it, just lying the whole time.

One of my neighbours went down to the police station with me to report the driving incident. A couple of times he crept into my yard and shone a torch into my bedroom window. It scared the me. I was home alone. The neighbours saw him in my yard.

Court was stressful for me and my family and the last time he did not even turn up. I thought why and how did he get away with this? We had to turn up every time to court and, in the end, he never did. I thought how could he get away with it?

We wasted our time. Mum had to have time off work. Dad did. I did. The court tried to get my ex-husband to pay for mum and dad's day's wage but he did not. They cannot make him. There is nothing you can do about it. You would think if he does not turn up on that day of court, the court would send him out a bill and bill him, but they do not do that. It stinks. He knew nothing would be done.

He was allowed to get away with it. How does that happen? We did all the right things all along, going up there to the court, wasting our time in the end. It is not right but apparently, those are the rules. The rules are awful. It is just wrong. The magistrate knew how afraid I was of him.

My lawyer was fantastic – she went to court with me three times. The lawyer did not even bill me for the last lot of work. My ex-husband started to say I was going around to his place. None of this was true; which was wrong. He knew that if he went to court and lost the case, he would have to pay for my solicitor that is why he stayed away.

He can be a smart bastard sometimes. He can play you for a fool and in the end, he did. I decided to let it go, it was not worth it in the end, we tried and we tried and we tried and in the end we had just had enough. I thought about going up to the court and telling them how my ex has treated my family and me.

Chapter 9
Staying in the house

After I kicked him out, I was very determined to stay in the house. Mum and dad asked me to come home to live with them for a while, but I did not understand why I had to leave. I had stayed in my house through the whole mess. I did not move.

My counsellor, from the relationship centre, asked me when I first broke up, 'Do you want to stay with your mum and dad?'

I said, 'Why? It's my house? Why should I move?'

I said, 'Just because I kicked him out doesn't mean I have to move. If I move, he will think he won'.

I decided that I was going to stick to my guns and I did. I was determined. My mother asked me to come home just for a week or something just to get away, but I said, 'No way'.

I had my dog to look after. My dog hade been with me through all of this, why would we leave? It is our house. My dog was protecting me and he was protecting the yard. My dog has been with me through it all and protected me; he let me know if he heard my ex-husband around the house. When my ex-husband first left, my dog stayed inside the house with me most of the time. He helped me feel safer. If the dog heard anything, he would let me know straight away.

The police were really good when I needed them. They were there in a flash and I did need them sometimes in the middle of the night. That made me feel safer. It made it possible for me to stay in my own home because I knew the police would come if I called them. He thought he would get the house, but my parents had helped us a lot in the first place to buy that house. His parents did not help at all. It was my home and I wanted to keep it.

I was help by many agencies including the domestic violence outreach service. The most helpful thing about the domestic violence outreach service was having someone to talk to. I could go to them to talk out my situation with no one judging me. If I felt like I wanted to cry, I could cry, and when I did cry I could just let it all out and it felt really good afterwards. I had none of that pressure or anger inside of me. When I did that, it felt so good after and I would think at least I have let it all out. Even when I went home, I would just let it all out again when I was speaking with my mother or sister.

I would listen to the advice of my solicitor and the women at the domestic violence outreach, then I would go home and my mind would go over and over everything. In the end, I just got sick of thinking about this. My mind felt as if it was working overtime. I think I got the help that I needed.

Before I started going to the domestic violence outreach service, I did talk to my husband. I said, 'Why don't you get some help? If you can't talk to your family go get help'. He wouldn't.

So I said, 'That's not my problem; that's yours if you can't get help for yourself.'

I said, 'At least I'm getting help.'

Now look where that help has got me. Today I live without any pressure or anything. Whenever I feel pressure, I have my family, friends, the domestic violence outreach service and my lawyers. He did nothing for himself. He said, 'I know what I'm doing, I don't need to talk to anyone.'

It was a difficult time for me and my family, but we got through it. You just have to stick together as a family. I hope we never have to go through it again. I think things have stopped now, since the divorce, but if he does anything again I will go straight up to the police station. I have changed my surname back to my maiden name.

My bosses, supervisors and all my friends at work have been fantastic and supportive. They have all been there for me. My neighbours have been very supportive. I feel safer now I know they are there to help. The police have also said that if he tries to call or turns up I have to ring them straight away. With this support, I feel as if I have no worries now. I am just glad he is not my problem anymore.

How my life is different now…

I got the house in our divorce settlement. My solicitors helped me organise everything. I had to pay him some money. My sister has moved in with me now. Having the house, I thought to myself, 'I have one up on you now'.

The situation has changed for me now. It is great, it is fantastic. I feel as if I have freedom to go where I want and do what I want. I feel as if I can go here, go there, which I have been doing and I do not have all that nagging. I can go out and enjoy myself, then go home to a peaceful house. It is just fantastic and I feel as if I have my freedom and I can do what I want, get home when I want. I can see the people I want to see.

I get a little lonely sometimes and I still get little down in the dumps sometimes about things, but then I get over it. My family encourages me to keep positive if I get a bit lonely just remember what it was like when he lived there. I am speaking to my neighbours now that he has left. When I was married, he liked to control everything. He thought it was what husbands were allowed to do.

He is in another relationship now, but he still contacts me and says things like, 'I have no life'.

I always think to myself: 'I have a better life than he's got. I have more friends and family than what you have got and your parents have even kicked you out'.

My friends thought I should never have got married to him. They said he was always a bastard and they know I should have never married him. I wish I had never married him now either, but I thought he would change for the better once we were married. I always thought that 'he was the love of my life'. You get engaged, married, but I would never get married again.

I said to my mother, 'I never want to go through that again.' If I meet someone, I would rather just live with them and do it that way. Why go through all that again. Half of my friends have been through what I have and they think why go through all that?

My advice to others

My advice to other women is turn to family and friends. I did. If you do not have family you can rely on, then find someone you trust and talk to them. Go to a women's service. They understand and are there to help you. My work sent me to a relationship centre for counselling, and they told me about the local domestic violence service. Women with disabilities, especially, need to know where to go to get help.

Part 5
Yulia Sukhanova

Chapter 10
Abuse in my marriage

From a very young child and all through my life I have suffered from depression and I did not really understand what it was. During my marriage, I suffered what I would describe as about four breakdowns and I got no help from my husband. The most severe depression, as I can understand it now, was when I lost my daughter (a miscarriage at between 26 and 28 weeks), the pregnancy between my two children. It was a loss, a death and a grief and I suppose I would have felt better if I was able to bury her, but I was not able to.

It was horrific for me, so I threw myself into my first child. All I could deal with was cleaning the house. I had a second child and shortly after that, I was diagnosed with cancer. I had to have a partial hysterectomy. The doctors left my ovaries intact. I had no support. No support from my husband and no support from my family. I am one of six siblings.

Not long after the first cancer operation, I came to the United Kingdom with my husband and two children. I began experiencing discomfort and pain when I tried to have sex with my husband. He did not understand. I went to see a specialist who operated and found cysts wrapped around my ovaries and bowel. I should have had six weeks off work to recover, but with two and a half thousand pounds worth of medical bills, I needed to get straight back to work.

I worked as a cleaner in a hotel. One day I collapsed in one of the rooms because I returned to work too early. The girls covered for me, which was good. I did not have the time to heal which was bad, but hey that is what women do. We sacrifice our health to maintain our households.

I had to go back for my six week check up and my husband wanted to come with me. I did not really understand why he wanted to come with me. I was quite happy to go on my own. Well, we were not in the doctor's office very long when my husband said he wanted to know when we could have sex. I could have died. I was so embarrassed. I was so proud of my doctor's response though.

He said, "Your wife has been through major surgery. She may not be ready for sex for months – it hurts."

When women experience surgically induced menopause they need to go onto hormone replacement medication. It is terrible. You get depressed and you put on a lot of weight.

My husband was not interested in my health and wellbeing. He was not interested in me getting better. He was only focused on sex. As a woman, I thought I had to have sex with him, but it hurt. It felt like my insides were ripping apart. I stayed on the hormone replacement therapy for ten years then gave it away. I thought ten years was long enough. It made me feel depressed and stack on the weight. I started to look at alternative therapies.

All throughout this time, my husband's only focus was on sex and this was a big issue for me. I would do anything to avoid going to bed. I would bake all night, clean the house, do my jigsaw puzzles, anything to avoid bed because my husband disrespected me. I would be heaving inside I was so disgusted. I could never have talked to him about how I felt. He would just start abusing me. He would just put me down. Back then, I was very quiet I would not have said boo to a goose. I was his puppet.

'Our relationship should never have started…'

I met my husband when I was very young. Our relationship should have never started and I guess I have always felt guilty about it. I was eighteen and had a full time job. I got some time off work and was holidaying with friends. We were travelling near where my foster parents lived, so I decided to get dropped off for the day while my friends went off and did their own thing.

My foster sister was also visiting our foster parents with her boyfriend. She was pregnant. At the end of the day, my friends returned to pick me up and they were drunk. I said no way would I get in the car with them. I would rather hitchhike. My foster parents asked me to stay the night.

Overnight, my foster sister got sick with the flu. She needed to stay in bed so my foster parents arranged for her boyfriend to give me a lift home. My foster sister, her boyfriend and I started spending time with each other on weekends. I would go over to their place and help out with the housework. My foster sister was not the tidiest of people.

There was this one time when I was moving house and they were helping. Well, my foster sister was not able to do very much because she had recently had a baby. Her and her boyfriend had a huge fight and he stormed off. Next thing I know is my foster sister is locked in the bathroom and I am looking after the baby. I was young and naïve.

She took too long in the bathroom so I started banging on the door calling her. When she did not answer, I just opened the bathroom door. She was lying with her head under water. I screamed and rushed to pull the plug out. She went into the lounge room, got out the yellow pages and began calling numbers. I did not know what she was doing. She had been off her medication for a couple of days. She rang an ambulance. She knew she needed help.

Her boyfriend returned demanding to know where she and his baby had gone. He took off after her.

Later that night he rang me and said that he and my foster sister's doctors were going to have her committed the next morning. He sounded so very sad. From the way he was talking, he sounded suicidal.

I picked up on it straight away and said, "Don't be stupid. You have a baby, a partner."

He said, "No, I have had enough."

He made me feel very guilty. He made me feel he was the one who needed all the support. I did not understand what he had done until years later.

He made me feel he was the most needy, but he was not the one locked up in hospital. My foster sister was. He was not a baby. His daughter was. He was the adult. Anyway, I said I would jump into a taxi and go over and stay the night in his spare bedroom. We sat up talking for a long time then I thought I had better go to bed because I had work the next day.

I went to bed then I heard something. He was in my room, getting into my bed.

I said, "What do you think you are you doing?"

I cannot remember what he said, but my head was spinning and I just kept saying, "What do you think you are you doing? What about my foster sister?"

He said, "She doesn't matter."

How do I explain what happened? I felt powerless. I felt like an idiot to have put myself in that position.

This is how our relationship began.

Now how can anything that starts like that work? How is that meant to be healthy? He was thirteen years older than I was. He knew what he was doing. I felt so much guilt. My foster sister's boyfriend! The father of her child became my husband.

After I had had our two children, there was a court case over his daughter with my foster sister. He would not testify at the court and I found out that it was because he had a criminal record. He had previously been convicted for a sex offence with a minor. I had no idea about his past. I mean I was very angry and terrified for my own kids. I rang a friend who was a prison officer. I needed to know whether or not it was true and it was. My husband had spent eighteen months in jail for having sex with a fifteen-year-old girl.

I also found out that my husband had been having with sex with my foster sister at different times throughout our relationship. I felt a connection with his family, I did feel welcomed, and the fact that they believed in this life ever after was an attractive idea to me.

Chapter 11
How I coped with the abuse

I coped with the abuse by avoiding the relationship. I would stay up all night. He was mentally abusive not often physically abusive. He once tried to drag me through the car door window with my daughter in the car. When the kids were little, I always had a hot meal ready in the middle of the day for him to come home to at lunchtime. If I got caught down the street, he would go off his rocker, yelling, demanding to know where I was.

What changed for me?

What changed for me in our relationship was that I found myself. I gained my independence. I wanted to learn to drive. My husband would not allow me to take driving lessons. He gave me lessons, which was a bad idea, but I was determined and anyway I got my driving licence. I wanted to be able to drive myself to places. I did not want to have to rely on my husband.

I was working at the time. I started out with a casual job at a Tesco, then I went part time, moved to permanent then got a supervisor's job. I thought this was great. I can go to work, come home, meet people socially and have a life for me. Then slowly but surely, I began to meet the girls for a cuppa before work. I was really organised with my kids in the mornings. They had their routine going. They were fine.

I think I just got to a stage when I could not take it anymore. Sometimes I would go to the pokies after work and I would be saying all the time, 'I have to go, I have to go, he will be up here any minute.'

I suppose in the relationship, even though I was developing some independence, he was still trying to squash me, control me. Life has to be more than just going to work, coming home and getting up and doing it all over again. You have to have some friends. You have to have some life.

Leaving my husband and going to a refuge

The week I left him, my head was just building up. My sister came to visit with a friend. They wanted go to the park.

I said, "You go on, I'll meet you there in my car."

I went to the park. I was just sitting there thinking: 'No, our lives can't be like this forever. It's too much for me. He's controlling and intimidating and if I don't do something, I won't live much longer. I won't live under this pressure'.

At the park, I was looking really down and my sister said, "You have to do something. You can't stay like this."

I knew I could not continue to live like this. I went back home and rang a couple of places.

They gave me information and said, "When you are ready."

I said, "I'm ready right now. If I don't do it now I will never do it."

I rang my mother and she told me that my husband had molested one of my sisters years earlier. That gave me more ammunition to leave that day.

I said to my sister, "Quick! Grab everything you can. We need to pack the car. I'm going."

My sister had been telling me forever to leave. She was my sister with the perfect life. She had the husband, the kids, house, dog, cat, the rose-coloured life. She just hated the way my husband treated me and how he spoke to me.

We would be visiting and my husband would just get up and say, "We're going now." If there is one thing I am proud of in my life, it is the fact that I have had my children to the same man; so they are full siblings. That day we went to a safe place.

My husband was to pick the kids up from school. I went to the school and spoke to the headteacher. When the kids came out, I said nothing. I could not or else I would have broken down. I had to be strong, but they knew something was up. They just knew.

The car was all packed up. They just knew. We needed to drive to a meeting spot then on to the safe place. My sister turned up. She asked me if I had told the kids. I told her that I could not. She called the kids and started talking to them. It was just so difficult to listen to. My daughter just screamed. My whole body started shaking. Looking into their eyes was the hardest thing. We stayed with a couple of nuns for two nights then on to a refuge.

The refuge was not where the kids wanted to be. It was not what they wanted. At that time, they had a 24 hour worker at the refuge which was a great help with the kids. I was very worried about the kids, but they were having supervised telephone contact with their father.

From there, we went somewhere. I do not remember where. They wanted the kids to go to school, but they wanted them to go to school with different names. They would not do it.

I said, "They will just run away." So I thought – What do we do now? Where do we go from here? We do not have any good options.

I rang the kids' father and said, "Move out of that home and I will bring the children back. I will only do it on the condition that you move out. I'm sorry, but it's not your home. It's where the children need to be to go to school. I will give you time to think about it, and if you agree, I will bring the children home."

He moved out to the house of his friend from work.

As soon as I got back with the children, I started to organise the house the way I wanted it, unpacking things. He just kept turning up. He still thought he could please himself and do what he wanted to. Every couple of weeks, I would come across his things. I just needed his things out, gone.

I rang him and said, "Come and get your things or I will put them out onto the front garden." He did not, and nothing changed. I knew I had to move out of the house or the abuse would continue.

I made contact with a family violence service.

We were forced to move out of the house and into accommodation over a shop. We had to move. My ex and I both had a car each, but he had secured the finance for the car. I had been giving him the money to pay for my car, but I started getting letters from the bailiffs. I went to an estate agent and said, "I'm paying £290 a week rent. I can only afford to pay £200."

I was later referred to Citizens Advice. They helped me find a three bedroom place above a shop for £200. The only problem was we had a cat. We lived there for quite a while. It was a new start for us and I started working again.

That was the start of the journey, but really I was doing too much. The kids were having one-on-one counselling, I was doing one-on-one counselling, then the three of us were having counselling together as a family unit and then I was doing Centre of expertise on child sexual abuse (CSA Centre) counselling as well. It got too much. Looking back, the only thing I did wrong was I thought when we moved to the property over the shop, I could cope with him (my ex).

I thought I was strong enough now and that everything was alright, but everything was not alright. Hindsight is a great thing, but I now think mediation should have been brought into it, to sort out a few things with the kids.

My son was very difficult. In the end, my son went and lived with his father and although I was upset at first, I must admit it was a bit of a relief. There was extreme rivalry between my son and my daughter. People would say, ' don't know how you do it.' But I love him. He is my son. He had problems, but some of those problems were from the marriage. You just extremely do your best.

He would say, 'I'm going to visit my dad.' That would wear me down. I would get sick of the emotional blackmail and I would say, 'Just go and ring him.'

My son then started demanding that he live with his dad, so he could have a dog. We could not have a dog because we lived over a health food shop. It was against the law and against regulations. We had got away with having our cat with us, but there was no way we could have a dog. Living together just unravelled over a period of time and slowly but surely, my son ended up living with his father.

I got extremely sick. My uncle had just died and I needed to go home to Ukraine. I gathered money together for the airfare. What a disaster. When I got off the plane I really was not feeling the greatest. I had lost quite a bit of weight and I had pain in my neck–so much bloody pain in my neck.

I went to my mother's house. She took me to my sister's house about an hour away. My sister was not there, so I went around to my foster brother's and said that I really needed to go the doctor for painkillers for my neck (I should have had the medication on me. I should have brought it with me from the UK, but I had to leave in such a rush I did not have time). The doctor tried to give me the wrong medication – I just went right off, I was not impressed.

Anyway, my foster brother took me back to my sister's where they got me to see a nurse. I was in a lot of pain and sleep deprived. I was standing in my sister's backyard, in terrible pain and the nurse came out and asked me a few questions.

I just answered the wrong question. The nurse asked, "Do you feel suicidal?"

I answered "Yeah!"

Next thing I saw the police. I thought, 'Ok, I'll be alright as long as they don't handcuff me.' I could not cope with that. They took me to a mental health hospital. A team of people were waiting at the door for my arrival. The psychiatrist tried to shake my hand, but I was not going to shake his hand. I had not asked to be there.

That is when it all started in there. I just needed the right medication for my neck to stop the pain and I would have been alright. Instead, the worst happened. I got in there and they started treating me with very heavy drugs.

I said, 'Hang on. I'm meant to be going to a funeral today, I'm meant to be going to a funeral.'

Their response was, "No, you are not going. The doctor said you can't go". I got thrown into a cell with a bed and told to make my bed. I could only crawl. My joints had frozen stiff with the drugs they had given me, horrendous drugs. I had to face a room full of doctors who said I was to stay in hospital for six weeks. I thought, 'No way'. I got access to a phone in a small room I placed a chair up against the door so no one could come in and started ringing lawyers until I got a pro bono lawyer who got me out the next day. I had an open return ticket to the UK, so I just left. That was a really bad time, but I guess anything goes in Ukraine.

Chapter 12
New relationships and family difficulties

After some years, I got into a relationship. I guess it's true when they says if you have been abused, you attract more abuse. I met someone who introduced me to drugs. I loved him and thought everything he was doing was cool, so I got into smoking a lot of weed and taking other heavy drugs with him and became quite unwell. My son had left to live with his father and I was living with my daughter and my boyfriend, but he was a druggie.

One day he kicked me and my daughter out of our home and we became virtually homeless. I went to stay at my sister's for a short time. I wanted a home to detox from, but she would not have a bar of it. She did not think it was appropriate because she had children living at home. So I went to hospital for a couple of weeks and my daughter went to stay with her father. That year, I ended up going to a mental health service. I was feeling so mixed up and I never got the help that I needed.

I turned up and they said that I did not have an appointment. But I did. It was really hard for me to come out and do it (go back to the service) and they turned around and stuffed up the appointment. I lost it, I just walked out. I was so angry. It was their mistake. I never went back because they let me down. I never got the right help that I needed. I was counting on them to get some sort of help for myself and my daughter and that just never happened.

A few days later, I started a relationship with a man who had bipolar disorder and that was disastrous. We went away together and he got really, really sick. He needed help, I could not help him, and the police were involved. The police found live ammunition in the van we were travelling around in. I came back to London and took out an intervention order against him so he could never ever come near me again. I have an indefinite order against him and that is good.

When I came back to London, I stayed with a girlfriend, but that ended in a serious argument where I hit her. I should not have, but I did. It happened. While living there, my daughter rang to tell me that my sister had committed suicide in Ukraine. I got money together for the airfare. I just had to go. My sister and I had a spiritual connection. We lost babies around the same time. We shared experiences. She had had a rough time of it. From the airport, I rang my mum.

She said, "Where are you?"

I said "Here at the airport".

She just hung up on me. I just circled around and around the airport. I had no money and did not know what to do. A policewoman asked if I was alright, then airport security. When I told them my circumstances, they found me crisis accommodation. None of my family was there to help me.

I went to the funeral. It was only small. I had to go for my sister and for my own sake. The family even had a viewing of the body before the funeral and did not invite me. I went to the gathering after the church, my other sister from London was also there but we did not speak.

When I returned to the UK, I went into a women's refuge in London. After this, I thought about my relationship with my mother. The hurt, the pain, the physical, the mental was too much. It is just too hard. I do not and I will not put myself through it anymore. I have cut off from her. I had to. Every time I rang mum there was something negative, every time, nothing positive.

I thought, 'I'm over this. I have to stop it. She's just going to keep doing this. She's not helping me and I'm not helping her.'

Where I got my first real help…

From the refuge, I was referred to Woman's Trust. This is where I got my first real help. You have to be interviewed to be accepted into their programme. From that first visit, I just had this feeling that I was where I belonged. Two women interviewed me that day. They spoke to me as a person. They said I could say as little or as much about my story as I wanted. They said all the women that stayed with them have a story.

I was asked if I could share in a communal living situation. I met some beautiful people there, outstanding workers that really believed in me. I had a worker that thought I was quite creative and encouraged my creative side. I was very comfortable at their centre. The workers there treat you as an individual. There is this feeling of acceptance. There is a strong sense of being in a women's space. I think that was the difference for me. As a foster child, I had had male workers. I had no choice. I really appreciated the opportunity to connect as a woman. We celebrated International Women's Day. I had never experienced that before.

The workers showed me that I could have new aspirations. There was the possibility of new opportunities. The workers made me feel good and whole as a person. They were the people that got me the help that I needed – the help that was missing all those years earlier. It had taken five years, but eventually I got the help I needed. It was while I was at Woman's Centre that I had to go to court as a witness in a criminal matter. They supported me through it and without them I would have never made it. They supported me to apply for crimes compensation.

While at Woman's Centre, I had another breakdown. I had been under a psychiatrist for about four years, but during my time at Woman's Centre I was in and out of the a hospital psychiatric ward. One of the workers at Woman's suggested I use my compensation money to see a private counsellor and recommended this woman.

I started seeing her. She is a psychologist and thank God for her. She was a lifesaver. I feel I was destined to meet her. I learnt so much about me, working with her. I had started cutting myself. I first cut myself when I was 15, but stopped for years. I started again during this period. I was finally getting really good help. It took such a long time, but finally it happened.

The assistance from Woman's Centre and my psychologist let me feel a lot of the built up pain I had felt over my life and as a consequence I started to cut myself. I really think it was a combination of a lot of things that had happened, that I had got to a place in my life where for the first time I was getting the right help and everything was starting to undo inside of me.

I was able to be free to let stuff out and my psychologist was able to guide me through that, telling me, "It is normal, it is ok. You're ok."

There were times when I was not ok, but she (my psychologist) was there for that too. She really gave me 100% of her time. Even when I was in hospital, she would visit me.

All of this has affected me, but it has also affected my children. They haven't known how to deal with it. Their father came to visit me in hospital. I was alright about that. I was on happy medication, so it did not matter. I was so heavily drugged. I do not know what medication they had me on, but hey I would be eating my dinner and my head would end up in my food. It was horrible.

I moved from Woman's Centre to transitional housing, but because of a number of issues, I was not coping and returned to Woman's Centre. I then received confirmation that I had my council property.

At first, I did not want to leave Woman's Centre. I was known as 'mum' by a number of women that lived there. I would cook roasts, talk and listen to the women. I met many women there that touched me on a spiritual level – real people, with real problems. It was wonderful to see women blossom while living at the centre. I can still ring Woman's Centre today, years later. There should be more services like that, where women can feel 100 percent connected – services with experienced workers who know the system and say things the way they are.

At my council property I have two good neighbours, one beautiful neighbour on the other side, I feel safe. I feel happy. I am near the shops. The beach was not too far. I am really fortunate and spoilt. I love my little place. I have been there for there six years now. The longest I have lived in one place, ever. I received compensation payment for what my ex-husband did to me. I used that money to continue to see my psychologist. It was such a relief to be able to afford to continue private counselling – my psychologist was my lifeline. I know my psychiatrist played his role because I needed medication, but now I would always prefer a psychologist over a psychiatrist.

I just figured out that at this stage in my life I am not meant to be in a relationship with men. I do not want it. I look back on all the trouble and it has always been that I think with my heart and not my head. Sometime it is good to think with your head and not your heart. Now I realise where all my weakness are. I really like not being told what to do.

Things are slowly coming together for me now. I am starting a gym programme, but that has been delayed by the Covid19 pandemic. I really believe a health body and mind is what I need to concentrate on. I do not have a lot of contact with my son now and I used to worry a lot about that, worry myself sick, but I have come to accept that one day he will understand why I had to make the decisions I made.

My kids are my weakest point. I have not had Christmas with them since 2007.

My advice

I have a lot to say to other women:

Communication is very important. Find someone to talk to. Take that time. It is important for you to be honest and speak the truth no matter how painful it may be for you. If you are not happy with what you hear from a counsellor go get a second or third opinion.

Women need to be comfortable and safe. Look in your local area, a good start is the community centre. Look for a domestic violence (DV) service with a women's group.

Honour yourself because you have been hammered by the domestic violence. It was important for me to find the woman's side of me. I think that it is important for all women to develop and trust their women's intuition.

Recovery from abuse is a journey that's never over.

You need to put new positive stuff in your head because the abuse is so negative you need to get good stuff in your life.

You will benefit from support if you open up. Finding the right support is critical for your health and wellbeing.
It is all about learning and growing and sharing with other women. Listening and hearing women not talking over them.

It is important to be listened to.

Part 6
Dylan-Taf Ben

Chapter 13
The 14-year-old's journey

It was the afternoon before Halloween night in the year 2010. I was a 14-year-old boy living in South Africa, naive and ignorant of many things in life. I prepared myself to embark on a journey permanently relocating to England to live with my mother who came to England from Zimbabwe when I was younger to create a better life for us.

Although the sun was shining with vibrant rays, it was still a dull atmosphere with some gloomy sad faces not ready to see me go.

Mesmerised by the warm embraces of my family as they prepared their goodbye hugs, I was dressed lightly unaware of the cold snowy weather awaiting my arrival at Manchester Airport.

I was shining with excitement as I sat quietly gazing outside the aeroplane window, filling my mind with many unrealistic expectations of the new life I was going to lead.

..

My name is Dylan Chikarango also known as Taf. Fast forward 10 years, I am now a 24-year-old entrepreneur living in England. I founded Taf Incorporated Ltd – an entertainment and lifestyle marketing organisation which aims to unite humankind in music and art, with the aid of some key spiritual philosophies which have helped me along my journey to live a more joyful and fruitful life.

Among other things I am also a DJ. I have had the opportunity to work internationally in countries like Portugal and Scotland. I won the Zimbabwean Achievers People's Choice award in 2018 and was nominated for the Zimbabwean Young Achievers DJ of the Year Award in 2018 and the People's Choice Award in 2019.

When I look back at the young boy who arrived in Manchester on Halloween night, hypnotised by the new opportunities before him, I am inspired by all the struggles he was able to overcome and align with his dreams and desires made known to his mind during the long joyful plane journey to England.

Even though I was ignorant to the magic of Halloween night, I feel its effects every day. The idea that you get to dress up as your favourite hero and get treats and recognition awards from people, excites me.

In this book, I will be sharing my story in England and the circumstances and experiences that led to what most refer to as a *spiritual awakening* and the transformation I underwent.

As we grow, we are taught to embody the truth that ' words are powerful', and we should read loads of books as well as journal our thoughts.

My mother always encouraged me to read. Soon after my arrival in England, she introduced to the local library where I got many books, the majority of which I did not read, as I would rather do something else.

Since I grew up as an only child, I spend the majority of my time by myself in my own universe which I have grown to call my *inner-verse*. However, my mother's stubbornness and consistent encouragement helped me to read more and learn from other people's experiences. It also led me to a greater understanding of self which also gave birth to a wider perspective of my *inner-verse*. It also helped me realise the tools available to me to reconstruct any damage as well as build other constructs which you may refer to as a *mindset* – a way in which you view and simplify the complexities of reality (*extra-verse*)

"Death and life are in the power of the tongue: and they that love it shall eat the fruit thereof".
— Proverbs 18:21

I have been, and I believe I always will be, drawn to esoteric knowledge and wisdom which from my understanding refers to information that is hidden from the public perspective and can only be known and understood by a few initiates.

However, I am blessed to have been born in an era where this knowledge and wisdom is now readily available to anyone with the willingness to take the initiative and find inspiration everywhere to be the change they want see in the world.

In contributing to this book, I was inspired by my struggles, those I saw in people around me and how we became triumphant in the midst of adversity.

In my studies, I came to the realisation that anyone who beats adversity does so with the aid of inspiration and anything we can call great, I have noticed, also comes from the same place. I now understand inspiration as inner action, the inner workings of God or, as I like to call our higher *cellf*, towards the attainment of the good which we desire.

As you continue to read this book, be mindful of the words you read. When you feel your mind drift to thinking into the future, or to thinking of friends and family, remember to bring back your attention back to the present, to be in the moment. Have an awareness of the subtle sensations that are activated in your understanding of *cellf*. In understanding my story, I hope that you also find the same inspiration inside yourself to share your own story for the betterment of humankind.

"Where your attention goes your energy flows" our thoughts generate electrical impulses that create waves that we can ride to the good we desire by having control and discipline in our actions, or we can let ourselves drown in doubt by fearing to act. It is important to remember that alchemy and transmutation are about changing the flow of life and using the power of thought.

Be-friend the phrase "mind over matter. Using your thoughts, you can integrate raw materials of lead – an undesirable element – and transmute into gold which is more desirable, but the secret is understanding that it requires work on your part. In the bible, we are taught that God only helps those who help themselves and works in us, as us and through us.

It dawned on me quite later on in life, but I always felt a great calling to serve humanity and that I was capable of achieving extraordinary feats, similar to Jonah from the bible who tried to escape from his calling to action.

Growing up, my usual place of escape was in television. I would spend hours watching fantasy shows of characters with magical or extraordinary abilities and able to perform amazing acts, in spite of being prosecuted for their gifts. I often felt my reality to be similar in the sense that, although I was aware of my gifts and talents, I always allowed myself to drown in doubt by fearing to act based on the assumptions I thought other people would have.

One of my favourite TV shows to date is the BBC's One Merlin. The show is based on the legend of King Arthur and Merlin the Wizard. Merlin is portrayed as a young warlock born in a kingdom were magic was forbidden by King Uther, Arthur's father.

Nonetheless, Merlin's vision was to create a world were magicians and non-magicians alike were allowed to live in harmony without fear of prosecution. The series begun with Merlin's mother sending him to live in Camelot as an apprentice of Gaius the court physician. Gaius became like a father to Merlin and taught him how to use his gifts.

In using his gifts, Merlin was responding to his ability to act which awarded him the opportunity to become Arthur's personal servant and dear friend. In the end, he was also able to make his dream of a world where magic was no longer outlawed a reality.

Merlin used his gifts to serve the kingdom multiple times without Arthur's awareness and without fear of the consequences. The courage displayed by Merlin inspired me to also want to also use my gifts to serve. Although my gifts may not necessarily be magical in the traditional sense, the magic of life is found when we act.
Thinking back on it now, I remember my sixteenth birthday waiting for someone to tell me that I came from a lineage of magicians and the disappointment I felt when no one did, until the day I took the initiative to tell myself that I did.

However, in the same year my mum surprised me with a Merlin-inspired birthday cake. As the saying goes, 'You're what you eat,' so since I ate the cake, you can say I was able to embody the same qualities as Merlin. I realise now that if I had responded to my calling earlier without fear, I potentially would not have experienced the struggles I went through to understand myself and be more joyful.

From the story of Merlin, we can also learn that your current circumstances do not determine your future. You are where you are because that is where you need to be.

Some of our greatest opportunities are born in the most unusual situations. When you think about Merlin's mum sending him to live as Gaius apprentice in the king's court, it would seem counterproductive if you think about the danger he was putting himself in by living close to a king who prosecuted people of his kind.

Furthermore, at one of the king's feasts, a witch mourning the death of her son who had been recently executed for the practice of magic, attempted to take Arthur's life in return. However, Merlin was present, seized the opportunity, and responded to his ability to act regardless of the king's presence. His actions were recognised and that is how his legend began.

Magic is the ability to, apparently, influence matter using mysterious or supernatural forces. The mind is a very interesting and mysterious force. Scientists have concluded that the majority of the human race only operates on 10 percent of brain capacity. The reason for this may be due to the fact that the majority of the population conform, being like everyone else without knowing why and fearing to act towards their own dreams and desires.

It is said in the bible 'as a man thinketh in his heart, so he is'. Using the power of our mind, we can influence events and circumstances in lives and make them more favourable using alchemy. Take control of your mind and allow yourself to act towards the good you want to achieve. You reap that which you sow.

Chapter 14
Everything has a purpose,
happens in divine order

I came to the realisation that existence can be compared to gravity in nature, in the sense that gravity always keeps you grounded and seems to prohibit you from reaching for the stars. However, in those moments while gazing in wonder of the possibilities before us, we find the opportunity through inspiration to fly high in conscious understanding of ourselves and achieve extraordinary deeds.

"Your mind is like butterfly wings; they only fly high when open."
-Dylan Chikarango

I have come to the understanding that nothing is random. Everything has a purpose and happens in divine order.

My greatest opportunity came to me after I dropped out of university to pursue a career as a DJ. Being a DJ gave me the opportunity to travel around the UK and meet people of different ethnic groups as well as share my talents with the world.

I met a lot of mentors who taught me more about djing and how to really serve. Watching Merlin gave me insight on the value of good mentors and how to find them. Although I may not necessarily have been born from a lineage of magicians, I do, however, come from a lineage of musicians.

I remember when I was still in Zimbabwe, my father was a music teacher. One day he took me to the school where he taught. I spent the whole day with him. He showed me how to play different instruments.

I see a lot of myself in my dad.

One of my favourite conversations with my dad was when I was much older. I asked him why he chose the name Dylan for me.

He replied, "I wanted to give you a name that consists of all the letters in my name." His name is Day Chikarango. While in awe of this newfound knowledge, I rushed to the internet to search the origins of the name Dylan.

Dylan is a given name, meaning "son of the sea", "son of the wave" or "born from the ocean".

Growing up, I did not have the privilege of being nurtured by my father's presence and further cultivate my talents. However, his absence left a void – a darkness within me which gave me an opportunity to discover my purpose.

As a DJ, my artist name is 'SmallboyTaf/SBT/Taf' with the slogan 'You're now riding the wave with DJ SmallboyTaf'.

I was made aware of the connection between my given name and the name I would use to fulfil my purpose. I have discovered purpose to be the light that guides us away from darkness and, similar to the stars, when we gaze up we discover all the possibilities beyond our current circumstances.

In conclusion, when I look back at my past, I also see the value of mentorship, leadership and peers that Merlin had, in my own life. The impact that both my mother and father had on my life made me Taf, the man that I am.

Taf is more than a name. It is a philosophy, a way of life.

Being Taf is about responding to your inner strength and ability to act towards achieving your goals. Similar to thoughts, music also generates waves which can influence matter. We often respond to music through dance.

I discovered that music originates from Greek meaning 'art of the muses.' A muse is a personified source of inspiration. Taf means to Think, Act and Fulfil. The journey to fulfilling your desires, which are our thoughts, requires you to act diligently towards their fulfilment without fear of prosecution.

When I moved to England, I did not expect to do any work. I thought this was the land of milk and honey promised in the bible. What I did not take into consideration was that the Israelites had to first take the land and build it in a way that would aid their survival, using the resources at their disposal. We now live in a world were a lot of us suffer from cognitive myopia, were we are only satisfied with instant gratification.

The majority are hypnotised by the power of mobile phones, televisions and all the new technologies, without taking time to look deep within their own inner-verse and discover new information they can share with everyone. I noticed that when I DJ, the crowd moves as I would like them to. I have more influence in my environment and able to share the joy and happiness I feel within myself through music.

Waves ripple and reach different parts of the ocean. We live in an ocean of motion. We ride the waves with our actions and are guided by our thoughts. Every time we have a new idea or new thought, it is called a *light bulb moment* as it gives perspective in darkness.

Djing was the catalyst that helped me to discover my purpose and helped to cultivate the strength required to share my story and serve humanity. As human beings, I discovered we suffer the most when we forget. Scientists have proved to us time and time again that we are capable of many extraordinary deeds when we put our minds to it.

In the bible, we are taught that our bodies are temples of God. When we remember that God lives in us and works as us, through us and in us, we begin to see all the great feats we can achieve. When we think and act, we have no choice, but to fulfil that which we act towards. If you think about going to eat and you act towards it, you will definitely eat, but the problem comes when we fear to act. When you fear to act, you restrict the flow of the thought energy from your inner-verse into your extra-verse.

From my short story, I hope you will find the inspiration to act today towards achieving your desires without fear of failure as we only entertain fear because of what we think others will say.

Like the 14 year-old who hypnotised himself with the desire of living a fulfilling life in England, I made great strides without the awareness of this knowledge and like a caterpillar, I was able to break out my chrysalis and become a butterfly.

In hermetic philosophy, there are seven great laws that if you learn, understand and apply them in your life you will experience a great transformation.

The 7 Hermetic Principles

1. *The Law of Mentalism – The all is mind, the universe is mental*
2. *The Law of Correspondence – What is within is also without*

3. *The Law of Vibration – Everything vibrates, nothing rests*
4. *The Law of Rhythm – The swing to the right manifests to the left*
5. *The Law of Cause and effect – Everything has a cause and effect*
6. *The Law of Duality – Everything has an opposite*
7. *The Law of Gender/Generation – Everything has its masculine and feminine aspects*

When I saw the opportunity to be part of this story of influencers and people making a difference in other people's life, I knew it was my time to act and the words needed to complete this book came to me as I needed them.

Remember who you are and the words you use or see around you, represent the tools around you that you can use to build or destroy yourself in the process. All that is created is created through love. Love is magnetic and attracts things towards you. As human beings, we are electromagnetic. Our thoughts are electric and they shine a light for others. Our hearts generate magnetic impulses that attract or repel them in our lives.

Love yourself, be the embodiment of love and share it with people around you and you will find more peace within yourself regardless of where you are, when you are and who you are.

Part 7
Gail Hannock

Chapter 15
The blinded, depressed girl

" It's quite a terrible thing to admit that you have been in two abusive relationships. Confessing that though, I must add that calling the things right names is the first big step in recovery. Ironically, when I met my second boyfriend, I was quite aware that my previous relationship had been abusive, but I was not able to realise that things were going the same way again. I wanted love so much that I denied all signs right from the beginning."

When I started dating my first boyfriend, I was a 15-year-old depressed girl with family problems. I had a weak health, poor self-confidence and it was as if I was wearing an "abuse me" sticker.

Right from the beginning, I knew that something was wrong, but my intuition was silenced by the hunger for love I had. Later in our relationship, I realised clearly that I was suffering, but I was not able to identify the source. It was standing next to me and I was calling it love.

Being in the relationship was like being locked up in a prison, being tied up and unable to speak. Sometimes when we were out together, I "disappeared" for the whole evening and curled in a nook. I felt better away from him, away from his mordant words.

My eating habits were never okay, but with him at times, I was not able to eat at all as he used to scold me in restaurants and even at home for "bad table manners". I was not a sociable person by the time I met him, but I was not a lone freak either.

Gradually he made me believe that I had no friends. If I had any, I would not introduce him to them because I was so afraid of being embarrassed. Therefore, he discouraged me from making friends and on the other hand, he criticised me for being a loner. Later, I read in a psychology book that this is called a "double bind", a manipulation.

I managed to develop a kind of bipolar life. In some dark moments, I was desperate with pain, and in the clear moments, I was able to write a whole page about my boyfriend denouncing how evil he was. Guess what I did with that page later? I threw it out and persuaded myself to forget about it. I guess I could read a whole book on relationships three times and I would never admit that this applies to me too. Love is blind, the saying goes, and I was blinded by fear.

There were many obvious signs that he did not care about me. He did not give me any presents for birthday and Christmas. He did not keep promises. He did not return things that I had lent him. I apologised for him, believing the excuses he gave me. I did schoolwork for him and he hardly ever thanked me. If I did not do his tests for him, he would fail. I was an excellent student compared to him, but he never wanted to hear anything about my successes. He accused me of hurting him and showing off. He was 'The King' in my eyes and the loser was always me.

When I got out from this relationship, I realised there had been even more serious stuff going on. He assaulted me physically more than once and often he would hold my hand too tightly that it hurt.

The worst assault was when he strangled me and pushed me towards the wall. I was petrified and tried not to make him more furious. He never apologised for this, and I believed "I deserved it" because I made him angry.

Then there was also a great confusion in my head about our sexual relationship. I thought that everything was okay even though I remember myself going home in pain and him scolding me for being too slow (He was rushing to the pub just like he did every Friday). He did not care about my feelings. I thought my sexual life was just okay, but later I developed a post-traumatic syndrome and gynaecological problems.

I remember he could get furious about just anything and start to yell and kick things. Once he called me bad names just because he could not find his keys. Another time I was helping him with his homework and he would not stop shouting at me. Was I the one to blame for his laziness? Sure I was. I believed that if I had behaved well, he would not have got angry.

We never argued in the true sense of the word. He had his requirements and I submitted.

It was the third Christmas when our relationship started to break. I was so afraid of losing him that I would negotiate his insane accusations and try to submit. He did not like that I am not a "sociable person" (i.e. drinking and driving fast with his friends), that I did not wear make-up like the other girls and that we did not have much in common (which was true, no matter how hard I tried to resemble him and his friends).

I negotiated with him and soothed him for two months more, but our relationship was ending. No matter how I would try to satisfy him, he became bored and for reasons that I do not remember, he wanted me to leave. I thought my life had come to an end.

My 'last offence" was that I cried in front of his mother because I felt very bad. It was 'agreed' that I would not discuss our relationship with anybody else including my and his family. He gave the reason that it really hurts him and I had swallowed it.

I was beaten, broken, but with that kind of faith that gives you courage. I had tried to do everything he wanted me to and it did not help, so in my foolish head I assumed that I was not worthy to be with him.

It gave me a certain light. I realised that if I had belittled myself to nothingness, and had apologised for things I did not feel guilty of, and it had not helped at all, then there must be something else going on. The pain did not seem unbearable from that moment on.

His brother told me after we broke up, "He loved you only until you started to demand greater freedom. When you stopped worshipping him, you were no longer attractive to him."

It took me another month to realise that this was true.

It was only two weeks or so after our final break-up and I managed to find another boyfriend via an internet dating service.

Chapter 16
From the frying pan into the fire

This new guy hated women and on the other hand glorified his best female friend. He always told me to behave like her, to dress like her, to be like her. When I got mad and told him to go and be with her, I realised that she did not want him. He never had a girlfriend before and he was two years older than me.

The trap was that he was so different from my first boyfriend that I thought he must be a decent guy. He was not. I trembled whenever I saw him, even now. I called him a vampire when finally, I broke up with him and that is precisely what he was.

He made me stay up late and tortured me with endless negotiations about "his uncertainty whether he wants to be with me or not".

He never had time for me and would rather go with his friends to pub to "help them solve their emotional problems."

This personality trait that he seemed to be proud of turned out to be an utter falsehood. He would smile at everybody else except me. I saw in his eyes several times that he did not really see me as a human being. I have rarely felt so deeply terrified in my life, although there was nothing obviously violent in his behaviour… but his gaze.

This relationship lasted for a half a year. It was full of power struggles. He used to talk a lot about various forms of violence, weapons and fighting and he had a whole hard disc full of sadistic porn.

This all sounds terrible, but I considered him a weakling, an unloved child who needed a mother. I tried to help him, but he wanted me to be a hot mistress and a totally asexual friend at the same time. In this schizophrenia, I felt lost and guilty.

This relationship ended when I met an elder man and became friends with him. It was bliss because I would not have been able to break free without help of another person.

It was quite dramatic. Though my boyfriend had never phoned me at home, he managed to get my number and called my parents to ask them where I am. I was scared to death. He even turned up at our house and wanted a word with me. He told me that he feels he has to fight for me and that after everything I had done for him he must pay me back. Before that he always told me that he was sacrificing for me and that I was not worth him. I told him that I no longer wanted him. After he realised this, he started dating his friend's wife.

I consider it a great success that I ended this relationship within half a year. Even though I felt very powerless and scared, I managed to get out of his sphere of influence. After several weeks, my health had improved and I had more energy. The post-traumatic syndrome is still haunting me from time to time, but I have never lived so fully before. I wish that all those who are trapped in abusive relationships will find a good friend and can get out and live in freedom again.

Follow your instincts all the time and listen to your intuition always. It is better to be embarrassed once than to get blinded for years gradually! If you feel something is wrong, then there is something wrong. Tell a friend whom you trust and who is not involved in your relationship directly.

On the other hand, be aware that nobody knows better than you do. Do not let anybody mislead you. If you feel terrible, then you are suffering and if it is not getting any better no matter how hard you are trying, the fault is not yours. Quite the opposite. The manipulator sees your efforts as a threat to his power and so he tries to push you back.

Conclusion

All the authors who have been bold enough to tell their stories have sealed their legacy. They have recorded, and contributed, to history.

They did not want to dies with their stories and their thoughts; in case someone, somewhere, will be inspired by their story.

Words have power. Please use them wisely. There's someone out there whom you could have helped achieve their dreams, but you are remaining silent and sabotaging progress. We should be willing to plant trees that we know we will never be able to sit in. At least we do that for posterity, for future generations. Previous generations played their part and gave us a chance.

Embrace the problems that life throws at you, because what you resist, persists, and problems and challenges have a way of reasserting themselves. They never go away. So we have to have the resilience to deal with life's problems.

The struggles and trials that you face introduce you to your strengths. Pay attention. How long are you going to wait before you demand the best for yourself? Tell your story and encourage others to tell theirs.

Printed in Great Britain
by Amazon